50 Things Funnier than Cancer:

A Hilarious Book of Light-Hearted Jokes

To:_____, laugh a little today.

Disclaimer

is for satirical in nature and is meant for entertainment purposes only.

Yeah, Cancer is bad, but have you ever…

Released a silent fart in public that turned out to not be silent at all?

Held up traffic because you can't park?

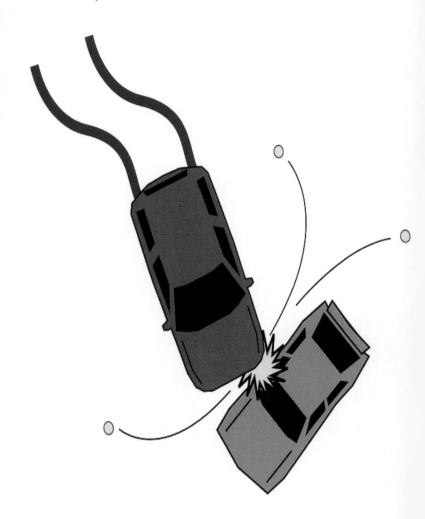

Clogged someone else's toilet?

Walked off angrily in the wrong direction?

Had a bird shit on you in public?

Lost a debate you started?

Forgot your dog's poop bag, so you just stand there looking dumb while your dog poops everywhere?

Unconsciously stared at someone until they look at you like you're a creep...then have it happen again seconds later?

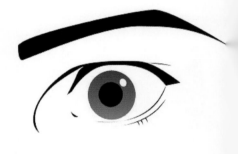

Been deep in your feelings, pretending and you're in a movie just to realize someone is watching you be all weird?

Waived at someone who wasn't waving at you?

Had your leftovers go missing from the fridge?

Had to sit through a racy movie scene
with your parents?

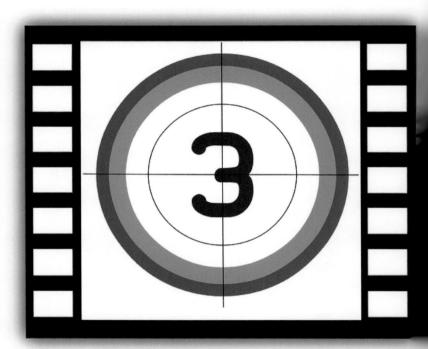

Not been picked for something you weren't even interested in?

Had someone walk in while you are taking a dump at school?

Secretly tried to take a picture of someone... with your flash on?

Called your teacher Mommy or Daddy?

Held up traffic because you are too scared to merge?

Tripped in front of someone you were
trying to impress?

Confidently shouted the wrong answer at the top of your voice in a full classroom, just for everyone to stop dead silent then laugh?

Had your card decline in public?

Held a handrail on the bus or train and accidentally touch someone else's hand?

Accidentally liked someone's picture from three years ago?

Forgotten to use deodorant?

Gotten caught checking yourself out in a store window?

Asked someone to repeat themselves ten times and still not hear tear them, hen slowly start to question your entire self-worth.

Been gossiping about someone just to realize they're totally in earshot?

Thought of a great comeback after losing a debate?

Forgotten the name of someone you should know well?

Held up a line searching for your credit card or cash?

Had your phone go off in a movie theater?

Had to check your phone for your parents' number?

Been paranoid that those laughing people are laughing at you?

Dropped the cover to the bottle of water you've only taken a sip of?

Reached for someone else's popcorn?

Have spit fly out your mouth while talking to someone?

Accidentally opened a message you wanted to leave unread?

Sang the wrong lyrics to a song...loudly?

Realized you've been heard talking on the phone about something personal?

Been caught picking your nose?

Hit a parked car?

Peed someone else's bed?

Had your teacher say they are disappointed in you?

Been caught talking to yourself?

Sent a screenshot to the person you screenshotted?

Had your parents cuss you while you are around your friends?

Realize you were singing too loud with your headphones on?

Had a minor panic attack during your class presentation?

Confused a person for someone they are not?

Accidentally mentioned something to someone that you discovered from spying on their social pages?

Forgotten your towel and had to escape the bathroom naked?

f you are guilty of any of these

trocities, then you have a lot to think

ack and laugh about...and what better

emedy than laughter?

emember:

"Cancer cannot cripple love, it cannot
hatter hope, it cannot conquer the spirit."
– Unknown

Printed in Great Britain
by Amazon

27178227R00032